ACKNOWLEDGMENT

Special thanks to Mathew Thomas for the front cover photo. Thanks to Pexel, Pixabay and their contributers.

Thanks to my husband David for all that he has done with and for me. Thanks to my children for their patience and help.

In the past, I have received prophesy from God, but I have never written a book about Him. This book is a book of few words it is the pictures that I present that are used to speak to God's creativity.

Barbara Harris, Author

CHAPTER 1

LOOK AT WHAT YOUR FATHER GAVE YOU

The first chapter of this book contains pictures of different things that God has put on earth. Some of these pictures are of things found on earth in different places. They were positioned on earth by God so that man "humans" would have to share or trade them peacefully. For example, some parts of the earth have pineapples, some have oil, some rubber trees, some silk, and some spices.

The pictures included in this chapter are of things that God has made, and you may have likely seen them over and over, but they are only things unique to the earth.

Some scientists dispute that there was a Creator. They claim that the earth just happened. Yet, in their search for answers about how life happened on earth, they have only proven to the world that there was a designer and that the earth, its treasures, and its timed and measured intricacies did not design themselves.

Scientists have studied the universe for centuries and have shown us, as of now, that other planets are void of life. They have proven that life on earth and almost all of the millions of things found here *do not exist* in any form on any of the endless number of other planets.

Everything you see on earth was made by God, even if it was reconstructed by man, from one thing to make something else.

Scientists have analyzed, dissected, inspected, studied, reconstructed, taken apart, sampled, transformed, and experimented with most of the things they have found on earth. They have sought to unravel the knowledge of how things on earth work, and while doing this, scientists have also found that there are things that men have no power or capabilities to control, do, or change.

Even though scientists have explored almost everything that God has made on earth, some scientists still do not believe that God is the Master Architect involved in the creation of all things on earth. They believe in what they call "evolution" and/or the "Big Bang theory."

For example: According to scientists, evolution is that a fish somehow came to the earth, grew frog-like legs, then changed from frog-like creatures to something else, and then that something else changed to something else until they turned into apes and then to man.

But, contrarily, scientists have also proven that most things that fall into the earth's atmosphere burn up upon entry. So, even if fish or man did evolve, all of the things you see on earth surrounding and keeping man had to be put in place or fall to the earth before, instantly after, or along with man. Man would have died *immediately* on earth if things like - food, water, oxygen, trees, animals, birds, insects, wind, and rain were not here at the same time as his arrival. All of these things have been *regenerating* and coming back *continually* over and over since man's beginnings.

Trees alone on earth have been made into thousands of things by man, like doors, floors, tracks, rails, poles, paper, tables, crates, bridges, containers, boxes, chests, books, sticks, boards, cabinets, shingles, rods, fences, frames for houses, toys, shelves, and furniture. Trees were also used in making the first: boats, airplanes, cars, refrigerators, and stoves and are still used for making fire and heat.

God keeps giving the earth new things to feed us and keep us alive through reproduction, yet, even today, nothing falls to the earth, as the evolutionists believe - except rain, snow, soot, or meteorites. And, even astronauts were not born with the protective suits they must wear to survive in outer space.

While things cannot just fall into the earth's atmosphere, things within its atmosphere are held in place by gravity. Without gravity, everything would float just as the astronauts experience in space.

If everything on earth was continually floating up in the air, as it does in space, we would live in a floating trash dump, ducking and dodging everything, and all of the earth's beauty would be destroyed and replaced by the chaos of all of the ever-floating objects.

God has engineered ways for things to renew and reproduce on the earth by themselves, over and over for centuries. It is magical that the earth, its dirt or soil, produces things that are sweet, like sugar cane, bitter like lemons, hot like peppers, tangy, nutty, sour, or comforting like coffee or tea, and a host of other different flavors to please you; all of these tastes come out of the same dirt, yet they are all different and besides this phenomenon - different foods are packaged for you as they grow - in example: the garlic bulbs, are double packaged, or coconuts are in woody packages and bananas - all protected.

So, scientists, contrarily, with all of their questions, theories, discoveries, probing, and facts, have only proven to men that there is a "Master Designer" of all that you see.

The following pictures are of some of the things God has given the earth:

RUBY
NATURAL PEARL
RED CORAL
EMERALD
YELLOW SAPPHIRE
DIAMOND
BLUE SAPPHIRE
HESSONITE (GOMED)
CAT'S EYE
AMETHYST
MOON STONE
LAPIS LAZULI

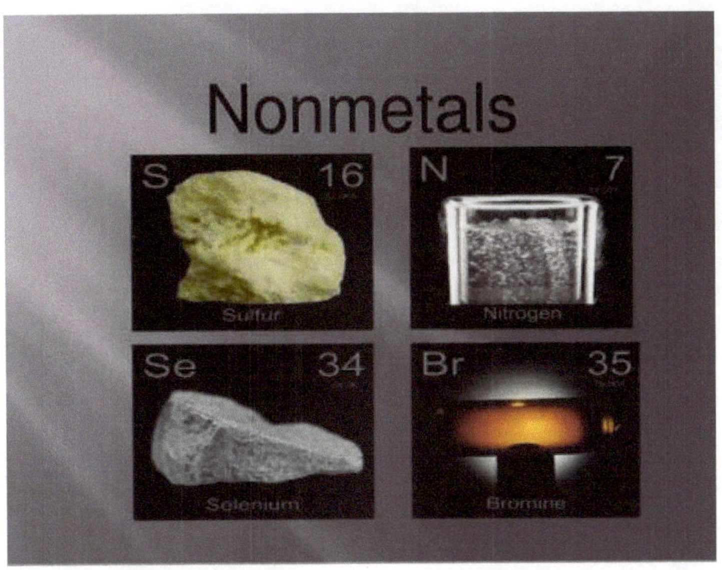

Nonmetals
S 16
Sulfur
N 7
Nitrogen
Se 34
Selenium
Br 35
Bromine

gray agate
moss agate
almandine garnet
ametrine (trystine, bolivianite)
aplite (dalmatian jasper)
aventurine
aventurine
azurite (chessylite)
green beryl
beryl
bull's eye
citrine
carnelian (cornelian)
cordierite (iolite)
dumortierite
goldstone (aventurine glass)
grossular garnet
tigers-eye and hawks-eye
heliotrope (bloodstone)
hematite (haematite)
jasper
yellow jasper
jaspillite
labradorite
lapis lazuli (lazurite)
magnesite
moonstone (albite)
black obsidian
pink opal
black onyx
peridot (olivine, chrysolite)
prehnite
prasiolite
rose quartz
rhodonite
rock quartz (rhinestone, rock crystal)
stilbite
unakite
zoisite (anyolite)

Boron(B)
Silicon(Si)
Germanium(Ge)
Arsenic(As)
Antimony(Sb)
Tellurium(Te)

Metal
Metalloid
Nonmetal

Rubber Trees

COTTON

BEETS

SUGAR CANE

Pottete
SPce

Mint
Sage
Origanum
Rosemary
Sweet Basil
Parsley
ROBERTSON'S
THE SPICE PEOPLE

SUN and SOLAR SYSTEM

PLUTO

VENUS

MARS

NEPTUNE

URANUS

JUPITER

CHAPTER 2

This chapter is about Man's progress.

Man's *progress* here on earth is the only thing that has taken place in an "evolutionary" or evolving manner. The Bible predicted that in the last days, man's knowledge would be increased on the earth. The accuracy of the Bible's timing in this prediction has been proven by the extremely slow speed of man's progress on earth over the centuries.

Scientist claim that man's time on earth has been about 6 million years, but - man - since his beginnings, has made a chariot pulled - by horse, then the cart - pulled by a horse, then coaches - pulled by a horse and finally, a car in the relatively recent, late eighteen hundreds.

In all of the centuries and thousands of years that man has existed on earth, he has only come from horse and cart knowledge to the knowledge of cars, airplanes, and rockets within the last one hundred and forty years. And until this time, no car, airplane, or rocket existed.

This chapter has a second series of pictures showing how man's knowledge, creativity, and early progression have increased until today. This set of pictures shows that even the things that man has produced came with time and design, and even – these things - didn't just happen; it took *centuries*. So, man's *progress* is a *better* picture of what scientists call "evolution."

Some men deny God but made themselves rich by selling, taking His creations, or doing whatever made/makes them happy, even if it hurt/hurts others directly, indirectly, or by depriving them of a way to care for their families.

Some men deny that there is a God because they don't want to answer to anyone for their actions or any wrong that they have done.

Some men think that they, alone, worked hard for the *things* they have ---- so, what has God got to do with it?

And, some men have taken, used, or sold everything God has made, even dirt, water, oil, trees, silver, gold, lumber, land, animals, humans, and almost everything God has put on earth.

God made some things unique to certain places, so that man would have to share or trade, but, instead of sharing or trading, men have made war over the things that God made, first within their own country and then with the advent of ships, men ventured out to other countries and continents.

With the discovery of other lands and the invention of gunpowder, canons and guns, men decided that they could colonize, overtake and rule different parts of the earth by force. They started taking lands that they never knew existed, acting against people who had done no harm to them. And this is how some men operated on earth, thinking they had to beat another country or someone to "it" before they did.

The only people God said He was giving His lands to were: the Jews, the Israelis, and the Hebrews. These were the "only" people on the earth - at the time – that He wanted to prosper, the only people not following or worshiping other gods, and who had shown God to some degree that they were listening to Him.

Some people worshiped other "gods," animals, or inanimate objects. Many people worshiped things that they thought maintained them or kept them alive. Or, they followed whatever excited the five senses that God gave them: of sight, taste, smell, hearing, or touch. Others worshiped the sun, moon, wind, or rain. Yet, if there were just the sun, it would have scorched them, the moon wouldn't have given sufficient light, the wind alone would have blown them away, and the rain alone would have drowned them; it takes all of these things working together to give balance in the earth.

Men, who have not wanted to listen to God, have wanted to believe that there is no God. They do not want to believe because they fear that they will have to answer to God for their deeds, or they think that if they don't believe, they won't have to answer to anyone and can use the earth the way they want as if anything goes. They delight in the things God has made but show no delight in Him.

Greedy men have taken things to build what they desire or tear apart God's earth, taking no concern for the earth. Many seek just to be rewarded one way or another by gaining things or, by the acceptance of other men. And, the children who are the beneficiaries of the goods gained by their forefather's evil actions take on their forefather's evil ways and goods. And also, take no thought for saving the earth or teaching their children that there are more important things than money, including God.

Man's actions are limiting his time on earth.

Man has created many good things, and man has created many things used for evil. Man's creativity is not the problem; it is what he uses it for that is the problem.

Yet, God has not tied the hands of men. He gave man the ultimate freedom through Christ, who gave men who believe in him "grace." But in giving man freedom, some men think that they are getting away with doing evil, but there will be a Day of Judgment.

The Bible's Apostles and Prophets guide you, so you will not be led to chaos and foolishness. The earth was given to man to enjoy.

God gave the Jews the Ten Commandments, along with swift judgment in the Old Testament, and then, He gave Christ, who is the Living, "New Testament."

The New Testament was for, by, and of Christ. Christ has given man time to obey these New Commands, which wrapped up all of the Old Ten Commandments in Love. Thus, "Love" covered all Ten Commandments: So, if you love someone, you won't do things against them, to harm them, such as steal, kill, and so on." Christ became the *High Priest* and the only Priest that might forgive and save you.

God gave only Ten Commandments, and, ironically, men did/do not want to be under the rule of God or to be judged by God, yet none want to be robbed, killed, cheated on, lied about, and so on and so forth. Yet, where God gave man only ten laws, they do not cry about the law libraries that abound with the thousands of laws made and executed by men, which they must yield to. Ironically, in these law libraries, men also include and then enforce laws similar to those Commandments that they claim to object to.

God created the Church as the working New Testament on earth. The Church is and was supposed to live the New Testament to bring its purpose to the earth. The Old Testament may be the foundation upon which humanity should have lived their life, but now the new law of "Love" that Christ brought supplants the rigidity of the old law with Grace. If any on earth are doing things that don't equal acting in love, help, or respect, it is not of God. He has wanted His church to love one another, work together, and grow.

Some men now call sex "Love." Sex is sex. And even sex is only valid under marriage laws, in a lifetime agreement between a man and woman; and this is in accordance with God and Paul's letter to Corinth.

There are religions that have been created to deceive or control mankind. They teach rituals and tell people what they must do, making their subjects the equivalent of robots. If God wanted to make robots, He would have made man a robot. Man, alone, was made to choose and reason. Animals, and other things on earth, are the only things similar to robots -- they can only do what they were created and purposed to do. Insects, birds, fish, and animals were made to clean, pollinate, plant, and serve the earth and man. But, they are limited in knowledge and can't be hired or used to be your banker or taxi driver.

God is the Creator; He is Majestic, Fascinating, and Excellent. He is Merciful and Kind. He wants to know you, as a Father knows his child. He has given knowledge in the Bible about what He wants in the earth; it has been and is up to you to listen, learn, read and do, and not be deceived.

The following pictures are of man's evolutionary progress:

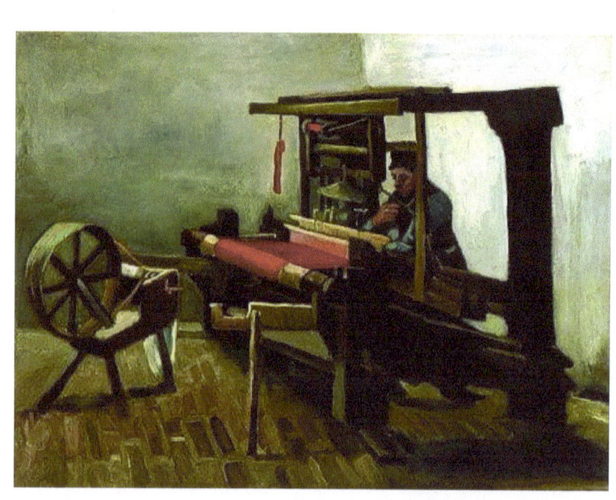

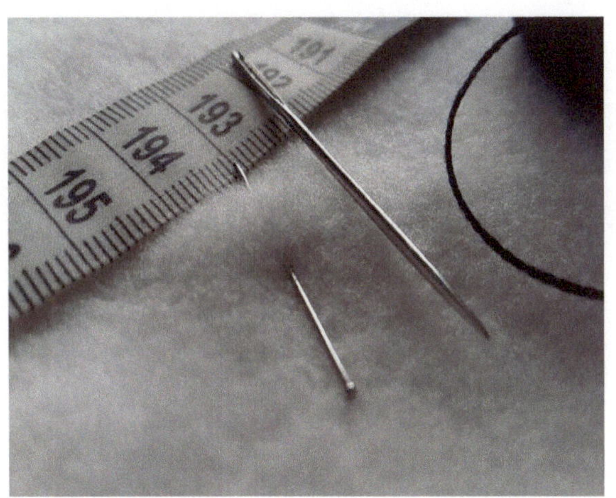

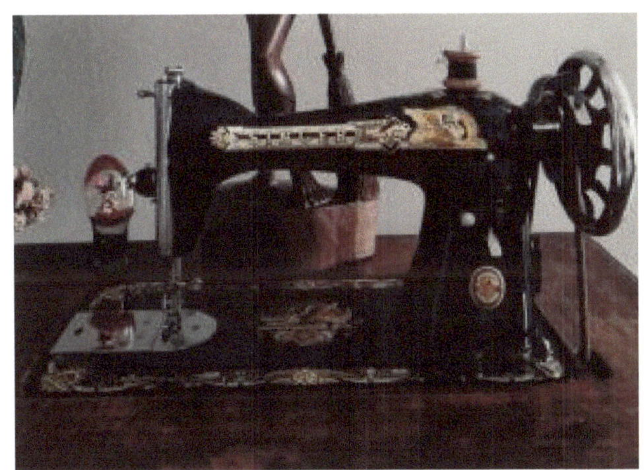

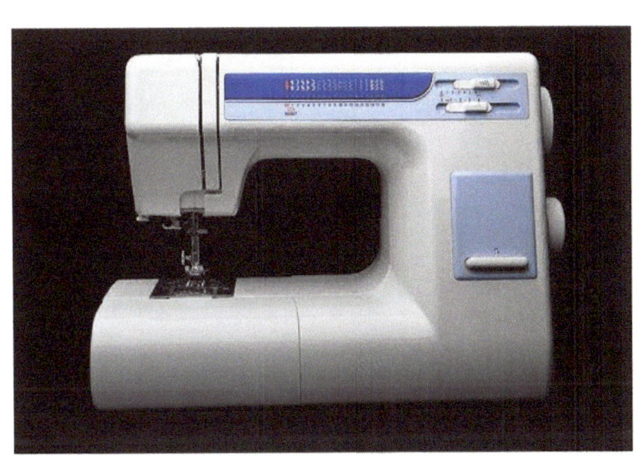

MÖBELTRANSPORT

DREAM OF
THINGS THAT HAVE
NEVER BEEN BUT
SOMEDAY WILL BE

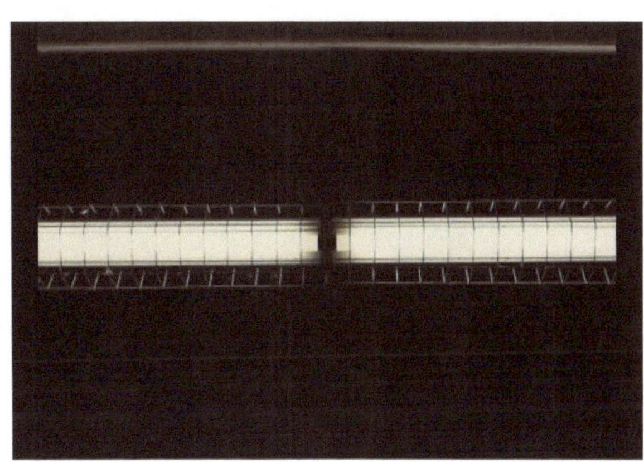

KEEP
CALM
AND
DRINK
Coffee

NEW YORK

ICE

U.S.NAVY
245